T0408885

ACTIVITIES
THEATER

- Written by Kirsty Holmes

Genius Kid

American adaptation copyright © 2026 by North Star Editions, Mendota Heights, MN 55120. All rights reserved. No part of this book may be reproduced or utilized in any form or by any means without written permission from the publisher.

Theater © 2024 BookLife Publishing
This edition is published by arrangement with BookLife Publishing

sales@northstareditions.com | 888-417-0195

Library of Congress Control Number:
2024952946

ISBN
978-1-952455-23-0 (library bound)
978-1-952455-79-7 (paperback)
978-1-952455-62-9 (epub)
978-1-952455-43-8 (hosted ebook)

Printed in the United States of America
Mankato, MN
092025

Written by:
Kirsty Holmes

Edited by:
Elise Carraway

Designed by:
Ker Ker Lee

All facts, statistics, web addresses and URLs in this book were verified as valid and accurate at time of writing. No responsibility for any changes to external websites or references can be accepted by either the author or publisher.

Photo Credits – Images courtesy of Shutterstock.com, unless otherwise stated.

Cover – bluehand, Ljupco Smokovski, sirtravelalot, FashionStock.com, Mega Pixel, Anya Melnikova, New Africa, naskami, Billy Watkins, megaflopp, Svechkova Olena, Master1305, Pixel-Shot. 2–3 – SeventyFour, royal akhi. 4–5 – TanitaKo, Adam bartosik, Adam bartosik. 6–7 – Christian Bertrand, Pixel-Shot. 8–9 – Chepesch, Mega Pixel. 10–11 – Nick Brundle Photography, Photographer_ME, kojoku. 12–13 – Kozlik. 14–15 – vikky, Master1305, Kamil Macniak, Ljupco Smokovski, GOLFX, Peyker, SimoneN, Pixel-Shot, Roman Samborskyi. 16–17 – Try_my_best, Maxx-Studio, Pixel-Shot, Pixel-Shot, Africa Studio, True Touch Lifestyle. 18–19 – Pixel-Shot, LightField Studios, Kozlik. 20–21 – Master1305, RichartPhotos, Krakenimages.com, triocean, g_hang.out, Katrina Brown. 22–23 – Master1305, RichartPhotos, Krakenimages.com, triocean, g_hang.out, Katrina Brown.

CONTENTS

Page 4	Theater
Page 6	Key Words
Page 8	A History of Theater
Page 12	The Stage
Page 14	On the Stage
Page 16	Backstage
Page 18	Becoming an Actor
Page 20	Believe It or Not!
Page 22	Are You a Genius Kid?
Page 24	Glossary and Index

Words that look like <u>this</u> can be found in the glossary on page 24.

THEATER

Have you ever been to the theater? Maybe you've even performed onstage yourself. Whether you like to be onstage, backstage, or watching from the audience, anyone can enjoy the theater.

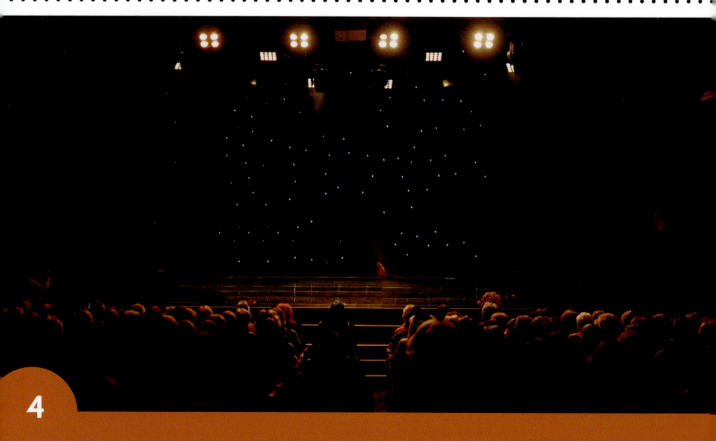

A theater is a special building made for performances. But theater can happen anywhere. It can even happen in the street!

Theater building

Theater is part of the performing arts. Other performing arts include dance and music. In theater, people tell stories by acting them out.

Street theater

KEY WORDS

Here are some key words about theater that every genius kid should learn.

ACTING
Acting is the art of telling a story. Actors perform in front of an audience using their bodies and voices.

PLAY
A play is a story performed by actors on a stage. The words and movements are written down in a script.

CHARACTERS

Characters are people in plays or stories. Actors pretend to be the characters.

REHEARSALS

Rehearsals are when actors meet with a director to practice a show before the performance.

DID YOU KNOW?
The director's job is to tell the actors how to perform their parts.

A HISTORY OF THEATER

Ancient Greek and Roman Theater, 1000 BCE–400 CE

Plays were performed outside in large, round theaters called amphitheaters.

Amphitheater

Comedy

Tragedy

DID YOU KNOW?
Comedy and tragedy masks are often used as symbols of theater. They are based on masks that ancient Greek actors wore.

8

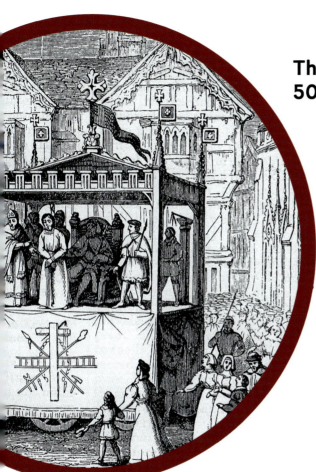

The Middle Ages, 500–1500

Most theater was <u>religious</u>. Actors performed Bible stories.

Harlequin is a funny character from commedia dell'arte.

Commedia Dell'arte, 1500s–1700s

This Italian theater was performed in market squares. Costumes, movements, and characters were very over-the-top.

9

Shakespeare, 1564–1616

William Shakespeare was an important English <u>playwright</u>. His plays are still performed today.

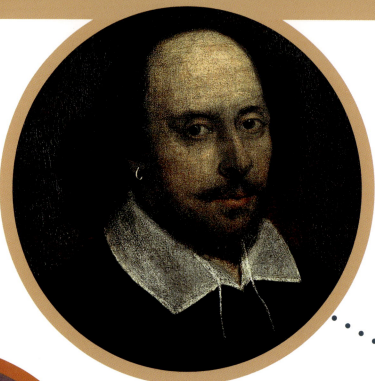

Shakespeare's theater was called the Globe Theater.

Variety Theater, 1800s–1980s
Variety shows had many kinds of acts. Acts included music, dance, comedy, magic, and <u>ventriloquism</u>.

Musical Theater, from the 1880s onward
Musicals are plays where part of the story is told through songs. Some musicals include *Cats*, *Wicked*, and *Hamilton*.

THE STAGE

What can we see in a theater?

WINGS
This area is where actors enter and exit the stage. The wings are hidden by tall, thin curtains.

STAGE
Actors perform on a large platform.

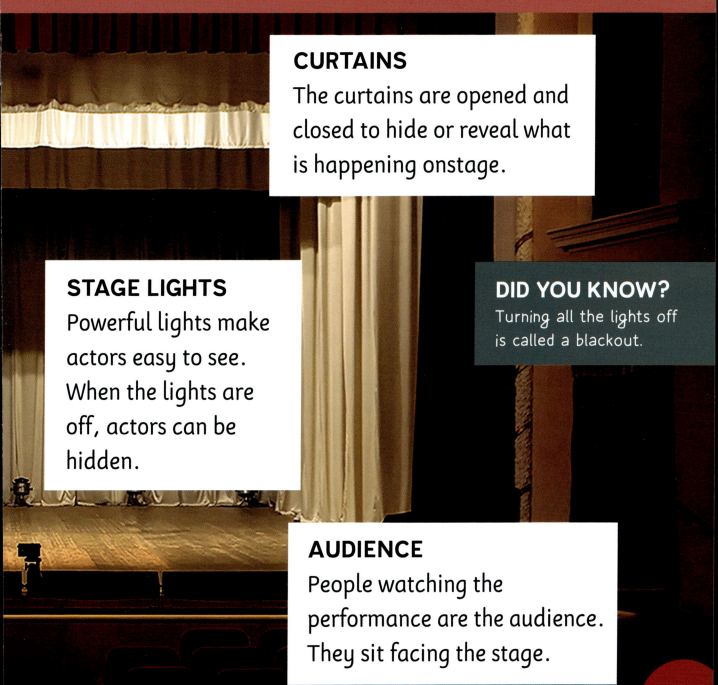

CURTAINS
The curtains are opened and closed to hide or reveal what is happening onstage.

STAGE LIGHTS
Powerful lights make actors easy to see. When the lights are off, actors can be hidden.

DID YOU KNOW?
Turning all the lights off is called a blackout.

AUDIENCE
People watching the performance are the audience. They sit facing the stage.

ON THE STAGE

Who and what can we find on the stage?

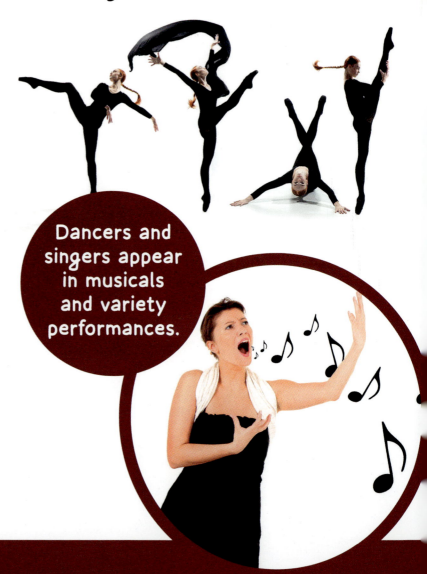

Actors wear costumes to show their characters.

Dancers and singers appear in musicals and variety performances.

14

Musicians play instruments to <u>accompany</u> the performance. They are called the orchestra.

DID YOU KNOW?
Theater orchestras sometimes sit in the orchestra pit. This area is often lowered in front of the stage.

Puppets can represent animals, small children, or fantasy characters.

Fake food, weapons, or other items that actors use onstage are called props.

Scenery tells the audience where the play is happening.

15

BACKSTAGE

There is so much going on behind the scenes!

Technicians work with lights, sound, set, props, and special effects.

Stage crews move the scenery and props on and off the stage. They open and close the curtains.

Crew members control special effects, such as rain, snow, and smoke.

16

The stage manager is in charge during the performance. They tell the other technicians when everything should happen. These are called cues.

Costumers make and look after all the costumes, wigs, and makeup.

DID YOU KNOW?
Stage crews wear all black during performances to hide them from the audience.

BECOMING AN ACTOR

Becoming a performer takes hard work! How can you prepare for a life on the stage?

START NOW!
Join the drama club at your school or a local theater group to get some experience.

GO TO AUDITIONS
Auditions are short performances in front of the director. The director decides who will be in the play.

DID YOU KNOW?
The performers in a show are known as the cast.

SHOWTIME!
Learn your lines and go to rehearsals. Then it is showtime!

BELIEVE IT OR NOT!

In Shakespeare's time, women were not allowed to be actors. All female characters were played by young men instead.

The longest-running play is *The Mousetrap.* The play is a detective story. The show has been performed around 30,000 times!

There are lots of <u>superstitions</u> in the theater. These include:

DO NOT say *Macbeth*. The play is thought to be cursed!

DO NOT whistle onstage. It is bad luck!

DO NOT wish performers "good luck." Instead, say "break a leg!"

DID YOU KNOW?

Instead of *Macbeth*, actors call it "The Scottish Play."

ARE YOU A GENIUS KID?

Have you learned all your lines? Are you ready to be the star of the show as you share all of your fantastic facts? Let's find out in the genius kid theater quiz!

Check back through the book if you are not sure.

1. What shape was an ancient Greek amphitheater?
2. What is a blackout?
3. Where in a theater do actors perform?

Answers:
1. Round. 2. When all the lights are turned off onstage. 3. On the stage

GLOSSARY

accompany — to play live music alongside singers
playwright — someone who writes plays, especially professionally
religious — to do with or about a religion
superstitions — folk beliefs about luck and fate
ventriloquism — when an actor speaks without moving their lips, so it looks like a puppet is speaking instead

INDEX

actors 6–9, 12–15, 18, 20–21, 23
audience 4, 6, 13, 15, 17
characters 7, 9, 14–15, 20
costumes 9, 14, 17
directors 7, 19
lights 13, 16
music 5, 11, 14–15
orchestras 15
stage crews 16–17
stage managers 17